Praise for Leaving Biddle City

"Marianne Chan's poems in *Leaving Biddle City* are ghostly, ghosts, and ghost-like. Even the language repeats and circulates within their forms, but without the frames of their forms. 'What is place without place? What is memory without memory?' these skilled and beautiful poems seem to ask."

—Victoria Chang, author of *The Trees Witness Everything*

"Marianne Chan's writing is all so tender and rich, deeply imbued with a generosity of wanting to share a place that feels like it could be your place, made for you to fit into as well. *Leaving Biddle City* is a wonderful expansion on the touchable, beautiful universe of Marianne Chan, and I am so glad to have been immersed in it for a wonderful time."

—Hanif Abdurraqib, author of *A Little Devil in America*

"In playful and lyrical leaps, the poems turn like pages in a photo album. Marianne Chan's speaker meditates on the meaning of what it means to be Midwestern in conjunction with what it means to be 'Filipina,' and through examinations within the prose poem's metaphorical boxiness and in dialogue with the speaker's community, the poems soar into ecstatic remembrances. What persists in this remarkable collection are important questions about the choices we make for love, and Chan's beautiful writing will persist as thoroughly as the poured concrete of foundations inscribed with names of family."

—Oliver de la Paz, author of *The Diaspora Sonnets*

"Marianne Chan's *Leaving Biddle City* proposes a rare and unflinching poetics of immigrant suburban life, inventively evocative of both the monotony and wild audacity of a demographic of experience that is at once mundane and vital, hidden and clambering for utterance. Chan offers a surprising and brilliant kind of anti-poetry, observing how 'all things beautiful. Become insufferable,' yet herein lies its power as an ode to the unglamorous inhabitants of an unglamorous city, that is, as an act of disruption to the mythical origin story, one full of failures—and also love. With pointed honesty and refreshing humor, these poems are for the ones who came here, 'found they'd been scammed,' and 'decided to build their houses anyway.'"

—Jennifer S. Cheng, author of *House A*

LEAVING BIDDLE CITY

POEMS

Marianne Chan

Sarabande Books ● Louisville, Kentucky

Publisher's Cataloging-In-Publication Data
(Provided by Cassidy Cataloguing Services, Inc.)

Names: Chan, Marianne, author.
Title: Leaving Biddle City : poems / Marianne Chan.
Description: First edition. | Louisville, Kentucky : Sarabande Books, [2024] |
Identifiers: ISBN: 978-1-956046-29-8 (paperback) | 978-1-956046-30-4 (ebook)
Subjects: LCSH: Filipino Americans--Middle West--Poetry. | Coming of age--Poetry. |
Conflict of generations--Poetry. | Marginality, Social--Poetry. | Memory--Poetry. | Sub-
urbs--Middle West--Poetry. | Middle West--Race relations--Poetry. | LCGFT: Autobi-
ographical poetry.
Classification: LCC: PS3603.H366 L43 2024 | DDC: 811/.6--dc23

Cover image is "Car Driving on Rural Road" by Marcus Bastel/Millennium Images, UK
Cover by Emily Mahon and interior by Danika Isdahl.

Adrienne Su, "Escape from the Old Country" from Sanctuary. Copyright © 2006 by
Adrienne Su. Reprinted by permission of Manic D Press.

Printed in USA.
This book is printed on acid-free paper.
Sarabande Books is a nonprofit literary organization.

  This project is supported in part by an award
from the National Endowment for the Arts.
The Kentucky Arts Council, the state arts
agency, supports Sarabande Books with
state tax dollars and federal funding from the
National Endowment for the Arts.

for Rammel

TABLE OF CONTENTS

Notes
Acknowledgments

Here in America,
no one escapes. In the end, each traveler

returns to the town where, everyone
knew, she hadn't even been born.

—from Adrienne Su's "Escape from the Old Country"

Leaving Biddle City

Winter Flowers in Biddle City

My brother in Biddle City. Was famous for making. The winter flowers bloom. He was fourteen years old. Was famous for making. A big fuss in town. He was fourteen years old. Football players watched him, a big fuss in town. This round-headed boy. Football players watched. As the flowers rose from snow. This round-headed boy. Didn't know that he was strange. As the flowers rose from snow. The crowds of people whispered. *I knew this family was strange. What's with this boy who loves flowers?* The crowds of people whispered. Football players tied him up. *What's with this boy who loves flowers?* My brother in Biddle City. Football players tied him up. As the winter flowers bloomed.

1

The Shape of Biddle City

Everything is a rectangle in Biddle City. No triangles, no circles, not a one. No swirls, squiggles. For example, this poem is a rectangle, and outside this rectangle is a bigger rectangle, inside that rectangular room are other four-sided shapes—windows, computers, televisions, floor rugs. Even the lamps are rectangular cuboids. This is not the City of Angels, but the City of Angles, boxy, wingless, no building higher than the capitol, no person higher than the next person, everyone remaining at a level height. Even the Biddle City accent is flat-backed and angular. There's a record store in East Biddle called Flat, Black, and Circular, but that's *East* Biddle. There are small circles as you move east. Today I'm at Driftwood Diner where I drink a square cup of coffee, a rectangular bus buses by, rectangular light enters through doorways. Rectangular people do not dine near me. I have my own four corners inside which I sit.

Falling in Love in Biddle City

My first kiss was with a snowman. It made my lips numb and tingly. Then, finally, I kissed a real-life person in ninth grade; we rolled around in pinecones. It made my lips numb and tingly. In my chest, a Midwestern heart. Come, we can roll along in the pinecones. I'll show you my hand, point to places. My heart was a Midwestern heart. With farmland, deep forests. Touch my hand, I'll show you places. Near the river where we can go. Within farmland, deep forests. We'll grow corn. Howl at the moon. Near the river where we will go. And I will wear my puffy coat. We'll grow corn, howl at the moon. While making love in the snow. And I will wear my puffy coat, and you: your pom-pom hat. While making love in the snow, my first kiss was with a snowman. And you and your pom-pom hat. Finally, I kissed a real-life person.

The World Buffet

A block from the Biddle City Mall was another strip mall and in it, a restaurant: The World Buffet. The sign had bold red lettering. We'd go after church and eat The World! The World was our oyster! The World was American Chinese food—different variations on sweet-and-sour chicken—sesame, pineapple, cashew, orange. We'd select what flavor we were in the mood for, scoop up some fried rice, return to our seats where we'd chow down, have a fountain coke, and gossip with Mom and Dad, sugar-induced scuttlebutt. This was always the best—the after-church slander of our friends. We'd grab a clean plate and get it dirty with our red chicken sauce, gluttony for $8.99 + tax. Is this what we called *renewal, resurrection*? Dad never minded the hypocrisy. He wanted his sweet-and-sour chicken as much as anyone. He wanted his green beans immersed in butter. He wanted an after-meal sugar donut—make those two donuts—under the fluorescent lights of this strip mall store. He'd worked hard for it. He'd gone to confession. He'd volunteered at the nursing home. He'd prayed seven rosaries. And Mom had not a single qualm. She went back for thirds, fourths. And this is *family time*, these moments of cheap luxury. We'd leave satisfied and a little nauseous. The World was our oyster, but the World Buffet had no oysters. This World Buffet should've been called *A* World Buffet because

> it was, actually,
> > one world: a Biddle City
> Chinese Restaurant.

Midwestern Ghost Ballad

My father lives in Biddle Town. He drinks Mountain Dew. He visits his aunt now and then, south of Kalamazoo. He drove two hours, arrived at noon. Cousins served cakes and tea. His aunt asleep, awoke too soon, and what sight did she see? *Papa, papa, ikaw na?* She held my father's hand. She thought he was her father, who'd lived in another land. Perhaps he was the ghost of Wong, the man who died so young. His aunt did cry for hours after, she was almost ninety-one. My father drove back to Biddle, trying to shake the fear. He saw a man who looked like him in the rearview mirror. Perhaps it was his twin who sat in his car's backseat, or it was a version of himself, a ghost on these Michigan streets.

The Suburbs

My father loves a clear day. In his cargo shorts, he goes outside, mows his lawn. Doug is outside too, arranging his gnomes and potted plants. My father loves Doug. He knows how to speak Doug's language. *Nice clear day*, my father says. *Sure is*, Doug replies. Doug's son now drives a red pickup truck. My mother made those kids lumpia every Christmas for seventeen years, and they would return the container filled with the snacks of their people. Brownies. Pigs-in-the-blanket. Those meatballs from graduation parties you eat with a toothpick. Now, Doug mows his lawn along with my father. My father mows his lawn in straight lines. Another neighbor, Jim, powers up his mower. There is peace and order in the suburbs of Biddle City.

Summer in Biddle City, 1999

Remember that first summer in Biddle City? That sweaty Michigan boredom. The sprinkler I dragged around the yard. The grass so yellow we thought we'd find phone numbers in its leaves. Television all day long. Commercials about Cedar Point,

the Power Tower, people dropping from 240 feet! Oh, how I wanted this: to feel a drop from under me that year, to have my body correspond with my heart, a constant sinking into the Michigan soil. Instead here was my eleven-year-old body, firmly

planted in a duplex apartment with you and a giant container of cheeseballs. Mom wouldn't let us go anywhere, afraid of civilian kidnappers, kids with guns. We had moved to America the year of Columbine, barely teenagers. Despite our mother's fear, sometimes

we snuck off anyway to J.J. Video for a thrill, bought licorice, gazed up at the new releases. We too felt newly released. When we arrived home, Mom made us sink to the ground, knees to the tile floor, a punishment, until she was sure we had truly returned to her.

Biddle City Filipina, No. 1

I married a good, American man, works for GM, good salary, benefits. Where is he now, he's outside. Shoveling the snow after blizzard.

With GM, good salary and benefits, we can send money to family. And he shovels the snow after blizzard. Would you like to take home pinakbet?

We can send money to my family. No, he doesn't like Filipino food. Would *you* like to take home pinakbet? Return the container when you're done.

No, he doesn't like Filipino food, only chicken, pizza, spaghetti. Return the container when you're done. Let's go shopping sometime, okay?

Only chicken, pizza, spaghetti. I make it for him, but I don't eat it. Let's go shopping sometime, okay? I know how to look nice for him.

I make it for him, but I don't eat it. Even though I'm mostly at home, I know how to look nice for him. I pray to God that this is my real life

even though I'm mostly at home. I see the snow on our porch, it glistens. I pray to God that this is my real life. I don't want to be dreaming.

I see the snow on our porch, it glistens. I married a good man, he works. I don't want to be dreaming. Where is he now? He's outside.

Summer in Biddle City, 2000

Sometimes, on weekends, we'd go to a community center and party with the other Filipinos of Biddle City. We'd play Aliens vs. Humans in the hallways, drinking out of two-liter bottles of Faygo Redpop. This was the summer of Paaralang Pilipino

where we'd learn to speak Tagalog. Uncle Rudy was our teacher, and we performed a play at the end of the summer. I wrote a play about aliens arriving in Biddle City, showed it to Uncle Rudy, but he didn't like it. So, we did a Tagalog *Cinderella*

instead. You played the fairy godmother because no matter what, Filipinos loved a boy in drag. The play was a success, and afterward, Mom watched the video of our performance on repeat, laughing at our flawed

pronunciations. But we never showed the video to any kids from school. Our only friends were the other Filipino kids in Biddle City. What did we think the kids from the suburban school would have said: *Is this a play about aliens arriving in Biddle City?*

Sometimes that summer, you, our friend, and I would lie on a trampoline, gaze up at the sky, and wish for a UFO to abduct all of us, slurp us up into its pop-bottle ship, so we'd escape this gray state, corn mazes, blue spruces, white peonies blossoming in June.

Summer in Biddle City, 2001

Our family talked all the time about the end of the world. Our father would say, *During the Three Days of Darkness, if you hear your mother outside, don't open the door, okay? It isn't your mother, okay? It's the devil.* You and I always agreed, we wouldn't

open the door. He kept candles that were blessed by a priest under the bathroom sink, so many candles. That way, we'd still have some light during those final days. But it was summertime, and ah, the Michigan sun! We made our own music videos outside

with a camcorder and the Filipino kids of Biddle City dancing in Bermuda shorts. Sometimes while at sleepovers with the Filipino kids, I'd have night tremors about the end of the world. Mom called them "panic attacks." Even if I crossed myself, I couldn't end

the bad dream. Oftentimes, I wouldn't remember them at all. I'd simply wake up in a different place from where I'd fallen asleep. Once I'd stood up in the middle of the night, ran around the house, screaming, *Hello? Hello?* You said you thought I was possessed

with one of the poor souls in purgatory, asking to be released. I couldn't sleep in my own bedroom for weeks after; I slept in the den next to Mom and Dad's room and had MTV playing all night long, a video safety blanket. I'd wake up in the early morning

with Madonna line dancing to "Don't Tell Me." You know, we never said: *Don't tell me.* Our parents told us everything they thought would prepare us for the end of the world. And before the official end of summer, I went into the school office for a Band-Aid and saw a plane crash into a New York City building, then another plane, and then an announcement, school canceled. Was this it? The end? I wasn't afraid, I knew

we were prepared. We had all the candles we needed under the bathroom sink. I wasn't sure if I should tell anyone at school not to answer the door if they heard their mother, I guess I didn't care much about them. I went home, we turned on the TV, waited for dark.

The Room Is a Rectangle

My brother in Biddle City locks himself in his room. If I could open the rectangular door—I can't, it is locked—I would find him there under a layer of blankets, a lump of laundry ready for folding. In this room, there are angles everywhere, sharp corners where one might tear a sleeve, hurt oneself. He learns early on that the body is a rectangle, a box that contains the soul. The box is pliable, can be torn on sharp angles. The soul would trickle out. He doesn't want the soul trickling out. It would mean disaster, damnation. But the skin bleeds and there were not enough bandages to keep everything inside: the soul, the body, the city, the room. The room's air is stale, a square of the sun's gray on the floor. My brother locks himself in. He tries to sleep like a lump of laundry ready for folding, his soul leaked out, his body not a box, but a flat rubber tire.

Autobiography via Screaming

1.

My family saw a therapist in Biddle City. *We're screaming too much*, my brother said. My brother was fourteen and sad. On the drive home, my mother said: *We don't have this kind of sadness in the Philippines.*

2.

The therapist told us: *When you're mad, count to ten. Go to the other room. Cool down before you say anything.* At the time, I thought that this would result in artificial expressions of our emotions, that screaming was the more honest mode. *If you're mad, scream,* I thought. But I was wrong, I understand now. Screaming was too loud. It drowned out all complexity. While screaming, we would, momentarily, not hear ourselves love one another.

3.

In the competition between screaming and singing, most people would consider singing the superior vocalization. Singing is more controlled and often beautiful, while screaming is uncontrolled and often abrasive. Sometimes at home my mother would scream, not sing, into the karaoke microphone, *I want to dance with somebody! I want to feel the heat with somebody!* Her voice reaching the garden outside. Even as a child, however, I never interpreted this as anger. I knew that this screaming was joy, despite it all.

4.

At church, the priest screamed: *Lamb of God who takes away the sins of the world, have mercy on us!* I asked my dad, *Why is he mad?* My dad said, *He isn't mad, he's just praying.* I learned then that prayer, like screaming, can change in form and substance. It can be quiet or loud, private or communal. Like in Romans 8:23, the spirit contains *groanings too deep for words.* Which I think means: the spirit must sometimes scream.

5.

When one of my uncles died, I received a phone call from my mother. A long, aching sound. It was not the crying I'd heard from her before, the demure croak in her voice that emerged sometimes while she told a story about her childhood. Her voice—in grief at the loss of her brother—was the engine of a great machine, low, murky, guttural: the spirit groaning.

6.

In high school, I performed in plays, which meant I was a new member of the sexually active. I asked my friends why people always screamed during sex in the movies. I found it as false as screaming on a roller coaster: *You don't have to do it.* My best friend replied, *It just feels better when you scream! Oooh! Oooh!* His eyes rolling in his head. At the time, physical expression for us came before internal emotion. In the plays we were in, we could make ourselves sad by crying. We could make ourselves angry by slapping the air around us. We could make ourselves excited by kicking our feet and screaming: *1-2-3-4-5-6-7-8!*

7.

After watching my plays, my father commented on the strength and loudness of my voice. I resented this because I wanted him to remark on my performance. And yet, perhaps, he believed that there was power in loudness. When I played alone in my room, my father would call to me to ask if I was okay and to yell, *I love you*. While screams can obscure true emotions, they can also carry them a long way and for long periods of time, all the way to the back of the auditorium, all the way to the ears of someone who needed to know what it was you felt, what it was you had to say.

The Biddle City Musical

I tried out for the eighth-grade musical. I did a monologue from *Crouching Tiger, Hidden Dragon.* I didn't make it. I don't think I was untalented; after all, I did a monologue from *Crouching Tiger, Hidden Dragon.* I think they couldn't see me. I don't think I was untalented; it's just that my invisibility sometimes flares up. I think they couldn't see me. They only saw the table, the choir chairs. Because my invisibility sometimes flares up. When I least expect it to. They only saw the table, the choir chairs. I think this is called *bad stage presence.* When I least expect it, someone says something funny about it. I think this is called *bad stage presence.* I tried out for the eighth-grade musical. Someone says something funny about it. I didn't make it.

Love Song for Ayumi

Ayumi never spoke in class, never responded to anyone who talked to her, and I tried talking to her once, no reply, but I loved her fleecy hair, her pants too short, not in fashion, ahead of her time in her high-waisted cropped trousers, and I envied the way she drew cartoon figures expertly on a piece of notebook paper, and I was new to Biddle City, and the year before I got there, she'd had lice, had already been considered dirty, infectious, contagious, a virus, so when I arrived, the White Kids of Biddle City with the frosted tips asked if I was lice-infested too, and I said no—but the truth was I'd had lice a few years back while visiting the Philippines, and if I'm being honest, I remembered that period fondly (my mother's warm fingers on my head carefully pushing her nails onto the white insect eggs on my scalp until they snapped), but I didn't tell anyone that I enjoyed having lice because that's weird, creepy even, because who likes lice, maybe Ayumi, perhaps she would've spoken to me if I'd told her, but she responded to no one, not even the teacher, not even the principal, and she was the only other Asian girl at my school, people claimed she knew no English, but they were wrong because she was a rebel, this was silence as protest, she never said a word, except one time in seventh-grade health class, when the teacher said *Ayumi, what do you say if someone offers you drugs,* she replied *Just say no,* the words as clear as the Biddle City sky in springtime, when it unbuttons its winter shirt to reveal the sky's bare chest: blue, blue, blue, blue, blue, and I loved the sound of her voice so much I wanted to hug her then, but she would've kicked me, I'd seen her kick other kids when they touched her, and I was a loser without a single friend, and she was a powerful girl, a fighter, never lowering herself, and

> I loved her, really
> I loved her, but I didn't
> want to be her.

Biddle City High School Theatre Kids

Fall backward, I'll catch you. Before going home, let's drive for hours. I'll give you a sloppy kiss goodnight, and before going home, we'll pass the dirt road, the blue-gray trees. I'll give you a kiss goodnight because you need to practice. On the dirt road, past the blue-gray trees, the church, the tiny farm, you'll need to practice your lines until you get it right. I'll skip church, the tiny farm. And I'll meet you at the auditorium. Go over your lines until you get it right. You can't dance for shit, but I'll meet you at the auditorium, and we'll sing and sing and sing. Because you can't dance for shit, you got a minor role: the one that sings and sings and sings. And you don't care, you'll love it, even though it's a minor role. Five or six lines is all you need to not have a care at all. We'll love you. You'll shine like a little moon. Meet me at my house at five or six. I promise I won't let you down, my little moon. If you fall, I'll catch you. I promise I won't let you down. Afterward, we'll drive for hours, before going home.

The Walnut House

We wanted our own place. So, we lived on Walnut Street and took theatre classes at the community college. Sam was a good actor, could bring life to Shakespeare, make his meanings clear. We drank walnut wine on Walnut Street

and invited people over. The house was owned by Homer, but this is no epic. This is a flat, nonnarrative, Midwestern conversation, the likes of which we had every day that year, the long winding talks a person could enter with little effort, a path in a field

with no hill or knotty roots. But I could make this an epic. I could build into it a journey plot, if necessary. It was 2007. We were eighteen and nineteen, and we ruined Homer's house with our boredom. Homer never came by

to pick up rent. Why was that? He was seventy and did push-ups on our back porch. He'd renovated the house before we moved in. He'd done all that work. And we drank too much and flushed tampons down the toilet, our friends vomiting

on the kitchen tile. By 2008, the walls in the Walnut House were stained and crumbling like rotting teeth. What is the opposite of an epic? A lyric? Lyric poetry is not the opposite, but just *another type*, another option. Some would say

we could've chosen *another type* of coming-of-age story. We didn't need the underaged lotus-eaters drinking wine on our porch, breaking the staircase banister. Didn't need the afternoons spent nursing the headache, bike stolen, the smell of smoke and Michigan leaves, the color of cheddar cheese, on our driveway. Perhaps Sam and I could've moved to Chicago. We could've auditioned for plays at the Steppenwolf Theatre. Sam was truly a good actor, could cry

on command. But maybe it could've been worse on Walnut Street. We could've died from raw chicken on the counter, someone could've broken a hip from all the dancing, someone could've drunk from the wrong cup, and yet, we made it out alive.

The Great Recession

I had no recess during the recession in Biddle City. I worked and worked and worked. I waited tables at a mock 1950s diner in the mall. We served classic burgers and malted milkshakes and had jukeboxes at each table that only took nickels. But it was 2008, a downturn, and we were supposed to depict an economic boom, abundance, unlimited Freedom fries, perfectly crisp. All of us were poorly cast for this nostalgia. I was a Filipina American with sideswept bangs, big dangly earrings, and thick black eyeliner. My manager was a man named Heaven who sipped from an always topped-off glass of orange Fanta, and who sold hydroponic weed out of the restaurant's white paper bags, delivering them to employees at J. Crew and Yankee Candle. I loved Heaven because he was always laughing and talking about the retail girls he wanted to sleep with. I too talked a lot about sex during that period. We all did. We were all receding in the recession; there was no abundance of personality or conversation, nothing much to say. We were gradually diminishing into nothing. Sometimes we'd break the restaurant glasses out of rage or boredom. Sometimes I made zero dollars at that job. Heaven had a salary, but I think he got fired or quit one day. I remember, through the windows, seeing the bright abundant sun of Heaven's self-medicated smile, bobbing toward his

> beat-up car, pulling
>   away from us, as he merged
> onto the highway.

Love Song for Kien

An Asian boy in my poetry class wrote about his broken heart as a bird in a cage. The poetry professor was an old, terrifying genius with an onion-white bob who talked fervently of trope, image, mythology. She ranked our poems from first to last. The Asian boy's poem about the bird in the cage was ranked near the bottom, for he had used a familiar image, we'd seen it all before: a broken heart, clipped and desirous of freedom.

Walking down the stairs after class, I approached the boy and asked him where his family was from, because our names both began with Only, and truly, we were the only Asian people writing poems in our class.

I'm Vietnamese and Chinese, he said.

And I told him I was Filipino and Chinese, and hearing this, he rushed down the stairs away from me, slamming against the crash bar of the door, and escaping into the blue-gray Michigan day.

Only, only.

Later, we became friends, and we'd eat together at a restaurant called Udon. We slurped noodles and ranked everything on a scale from one to twenty, including people, including types of Asians (the Filipinos and Vietnamese being at the bottom), because we were cruel and we wanted to be punished, our hearts broken as wing-clipped birds, and our poems with familiar beginnings and endings.

*

I did not hate the Asian boy whose heart was a bird in a cage. 27
Even if I'd seen that bird before, its feathers made a mosaic pattern of bright colors against its frame.

Snow Haiku

All things beautiful. Become insufferable. March slush in my yard.

Leaving Biddle City

Outside the Quality Dairy, pink-haired humans in their twenties sip on gallons of apple cider vinegar. This is where the sky is gray and the streets are gray and the message inside us to escape the cold remains unread. I want to discard this paczki. I want to crack open the sky into a frying pan and eat it with bacon for lunch. Once I saw a barn on fire in an empty field, filling the gray sky with more gray, smoke and ash, but also orange—the blaze and heat stinging my cheeks and lungs. No animal was harmed. The horses with their worn-out hooves galloped across the state of Michigan to Canada, gorging on cherries, chomping on boxes of Jiffy Corn Muffin Mix. Their need to escape belting the high notes from their chests. Biddle City, I'll call you my brief and little home, but the crab apples soured on my lover's lawn and I am tired of the colorless winters, the only-occasional fire that made me feel like I was somewhere, someone.

2

Autobiography via Revision

Years ago, a professor
read a revision of a poem I wrote

about Biddle City. She said: *Don't revise*

now. Keep writing new poems.
Trying new things is how you find a voice.

I knew she was right, but I'll admit:

I don't think I ever learned how to revise

a poem. When a poem isn't working,
I only know how to leave it behind,

write a new one, move on. Start again
on a new page. New place. New town.

New form entirely. This poem,
for example, is a totally new poem.

I threw the old ones in the trash.

A friend reads my new poems about Biddle City.

She's mad at all the pantoums. *So repetitive*,
she says with tired eyes. She's right.

I was trying to repeat the same old lines
until I arrived somewhere else. Instead,

I pedaled so hard that I dug a hole
in the middle of Biddle City. I'm stuck here
now watching the homely ducks

waft along the river. Why did I begin
this poem anyway? I wanted to write the story

of my life, my autobiography.

But what was the story?

What is my Biddle City?

♦

This is the origin story of our town:
In 1835, two brothers from Lansing, New York,
sold the land where Lansing, Michigan, currently is.
They called the land *Biddle City*.

Two brothers from Lansing, New York,
advertised streets, a church, a public square.
They called the land *Biddle City*.
They gave names to streets that didn't exist.

People expected a street, a church, a public square.
But they'd found they'd been scammed.
That the streets with names didn't exist.
They were in a floodplain, underwater.

Some who found they'd been scammed
decided to build their houses there anyway.
They found themselves underwater.
But they created a home in Biddle City.

They decided to build their houses anyway.
On the land where Lansing currently is.
Our home, Biddle City, was created by suckers.
And this is the origin story of our town.

◆

We were a family in Biddle City

who fought all the time
in ways that would make

other families laugh.

My brother pulled my hair,

bonked me on the head, a slap-
stick comedy. A laugh track

resounded from our television.

Were they laughing at us,
or the extremely unfunny

sitcom family that never screamed

or hit or smacked, only talked
at a reasonable volume

with sentimental music behind
them, hugs and tears?

I felt our family was underrepresented

on television, not only because
there were no Asians,

but also because none
of these sitcom people

ever fought with our family's specific
awkward ferocity,

Dad with bulging eyes,

his tongue curled under his teeth

like a piece of bologna.
Mom in her pink duster

slipping off her
flip-flop, pointing it at us

for the threat or attack.

Brother kicking a wall, leaving
a dent there, an exact imprint

of his foot. Me, trying
to punch a wall, hurting my hand.

Once our parents chased

each other around the kitchen island,
Tom-and-Jerry style, Mom threw

an orange at Dad's head, which bounced
off his shoulder, and Dad threw

a banana at Mom and she caught it

in her hands, mushed and bruised
into pudding, until we all fell

(in a floodplain, underwater)

gasping for air, laughing.

And I wished that they all ended

that way, a food fight, our stressed-out
parents finally seeing the humor

in this life. *Biddle City is a joke!*

I wanted to scream. *Can't you see—*
My brother was so fed up, he ran away.

He was always threatening to run away,

but this time, he really left.

He wanted to be just a regular
American kid, Fred Savage

in *The Wonder Years*, with stiff hair,

a cool bike, a few friends, a tall girl
with bangs to crush on, comic books

and MTV. He walked all the way

from the suburbs down Old 27

with bad shoes and a backpack
full of books, leaving

Biddle City, leaving us
all behind, his family,

the gaggle of weirdos. He ended up

on Lake Lansing Road,

in a Chinese restaurant, Kamp Bo,
where he finally called Mom

to pick him up. It's only now

as I write this that I see how funny,

how hilarious, that he ended up
in Kamp Bo, the restaurant

with the delicious shrimp fried rice,

eggrolls that weren't as good
as Mom's lumpia,

but good enough. The boy
wanted to be just another

American white kid, but he

ended up in a Chinese restaurant.

Couldn't escape the Asians.
That's where he surrendered, raising

a white flag. He asked

to use their phone, and they let him.

(Laugh track.)

◆

My brother and I talk about Biddle City all the time now.

Each time, we think of something new to remember.

We say: *What the hell? What the hell?*

What a hell it was—

But that is the story we tell ourselves,

that things were terrible in Biddle City.

Am I feeling sorry for us? I don't feel sorry at all.

I'm a writer. He's a comedian.

Together, my brother and I can revise the story,

we've got full control of the laugh track button,

push it whenever we please.

◆

My brother revised himself into a comedy.

When we first moved to Biddle City, my round face was covered in pimples. I wore big circular glasses, a tight shirt around my fleshy belly, and had not a single friend.

My brother said he made friends by making people laugh. *How?*

He said he made fun of himself.

If someone called me fat, I'd jiggle my belly. If someone asked if I was Chinese, I'd pretend to speak Chinese, and they'd laugh.

When someone called him *chink*, he accepted the moniker—

to tell them that he had something in common with them, that he too saw he was different, that he too hated himself for it.

(Laugh track.)

A local library employee says Biddle City is a made-up story.

He claims that Daniel Buck, a respected Lansing resident, mayor, and coffin manufacturer, told this story in the *Lansing Journal* in 1904, saying his father was among the men conned by the brothers from Lansing, New York.

But the brothers were not con artists, according to the library employee; they were well-established businessmen who sold plots of land to people in the Midwest.

Buck's story spread, later published in the *Michigan Pioneer* papers and then published again in the *Lansing Journal*, and *the facts change a little bit with each iteration.*

It is now on Lansing's Wikipedia page, written as if the story were true.

Maybe I should revise it. Maybe I should get rid of Biddle City, but I think it is more honest to keep it going, this myth of a myth of my town.

◆

And I asked my brother: *Why did we fight so much when we first moved to Biddle City?*

We had a story of our lives that didn't match up with our parents' story, he said.

And we couldn't revise it—

◆

And we have a lot in common

with the scammed people who came and built a life

in Biddle City. Like them, it was not an America

we expected. I call our hometown *Biddle City*

because the story of Biddle City is ours.

My brother's story, our memory of it, changed

with each iteration.

Biddle City is a town owned and built by us,

the suckers. Now, I live somewhere else entirely.

Always moving. Always starting over.

New place. New poem.

3

A Revision

Perhaps Biddle City was   the mind

when cleared

how wild the territory was.

From the *Lansing State Journal.* Sunday, March 20, 1955. Page 56.

In the Philippines, I was not allowed to go to college in a different island. All my brothers went to the city. *Because you're a girl,* they said. *You're going to stay with us.* This was my only way to get out. I'll be honest with you—this was my chance. I was twenty-two. Coming from the Philippines, I couldn't tell you what Michigan was. I had no idea. (I just knew, at the time, in the early nineties, the Detroit Pistons were the champions, so I said I want to go there to watch Isiah Thomas!) I drove everywhere—all over Michigan, then some parts of Arkansas, then Missouri. It was adventure! All my income I gave to the telephone company because I called home all the time, so my phone bill was like, oh my god, $600 a month, just so I can tell them I'm okay. They'd say, *Are you okay there, are you eating, what's your lunch* . . . My first assignment was in the Flint area. I traveled alone. Most of our clients were old. In their sixties, Medicare patients. One time I met a patient who didn't want to work with me because they, or their father, fought against the Filipinos in a war. I can't remember which one. I said I was not born then. We ended up working together. He was apologetic. I told him, no, it doesn't affect me because my conscience is clear. I did not cause the war. I learned that as long as you have gas in your car and a map and it's daylight, you'd be fine. Ask directions from gas stations. We didn't have GPS, we didn't have cell phones, okay? So, the only thing that gave me company was a Rand McNally, big book of maps in the US. Before I leave my apartment, I would highlight each highway I needed to go. I learned to read maps, so that I can determine where I'm going. That was the only life I knew I had to do. I do homecare now, still driving all over, even if you have a snowstorm—

When it snows   I know how

to navigate the roads   to shovel

my driveway   I pave

a way   pump my brakes   over ice.

Let's Talk for a Moment

about the persistence of ice, my father, in Michigan,
trying to manipulate frozen water for months

in his driveway. I can picture him now in his snowsuit,
thick gloves and boots: plowing, shoveling, scraping.

Different types of ice occur depending on speed,
location: *drift* which floats on the ocean, *anchor*

at the bottom of the sea, *freezing rain* that icifies mid-fall,
icicles weeping down store awnings, sharpened

into skewers. Sometimes I dream about the *rime*
I scraped for years off my windshield, that layer

of solid fog, a pest in the Michigan morning,
when I was running late for Russian class, repeating

the rhyming Pushkin lines I needed to learn that day:
Мороз и солнце; день чудесный! Еще ты дремлешь,

друг Прелестный! I'd say over and over. And there
were other times when I was injured by ice,

slipping as a child and bursting into tears.
Crying is a sort of melting. We're all hard ice before

a sudden pain or fear splashes its sun against our
coolness. I remember when my great-grandmother was

on her deathbed, I saw my father cry for the first time,
an avalanche of snow tumbling forward. He rested

his forehead against his inner elbow, leaning against
the bed where she lay. Moments later, he returned

to his habitual stillness. After a few days, I told him
that I'd seen him crying, and he denied it, not wanting

to talk about the warm waters swelling underneath,
not wanting me to know of them. Ice is a quiet,

fragile strength. Lately, I too am held together
by a cold so feeble I can break apart any minute.

But let's not talk about me. Let's talk again about snow
and ice, my father in his driveway, an immigrant

to America, laboring over American ice, spooning it up,
like cold rice for breakfast, into a pile in his corner

of the suburbs; let's talk about my father, who says
he's not afraid of springtime, hate crimes

against Asians, who tells me he always feels safe
in his city, where he can stay inside his home,

barricaded by snow, avoid other people; my father,
who asks for a door camera for Christmas, who watches

Forensic Files, learns all the different ways one can
get lost or lose someone; let's talk about the emails

my father sends to my brother and me, a list of his life
insurance, he says, *It's time to think about eternity*.

When I think of eternity, I always think of ice, the glaciers
which persist for centuries, seracs and crevasses.

It is April, and my mother sends me a picture of their
deck covered in snow. I imagine my father sliding

on his boots, drifting quietly outside to see his wintery
spring, his ungloved hands anchored in his pockets,

his eyes raised to heaven, waiting for more.

A Visit to the Suburbs, 2021

After years away from Biddle City, I arrive, and my mother lets me in through the garage door, then closes the garage door, then shuts and locks the door to the garage that leads into the kitchen. I don't enter through the front door because it's difficult to walk through with all the locks. The lock on their storm door takes several turns, and then you must unlock the top and bottom lock of the main front door. On their back porch, there's a sliding door that locks, plus a wooden peg that holds the door closed, as well as a screen door that's also kept locked. As it gets darker, my father shuts the curtains so no one can look in. At dinner, I ask my parents about Biddle City, and they say they'd never heard of it. They say moving to the States, to Michigan from Germany, was easy. My mother says: *Walang problema at all.* My father says: *The problem was years before, in Virginia, I could barely speak English, shared one car with my six brothers, washed dishes at Domino's Pizza.* We spend the evening watching Tagalog teleseries. As we get ready for bed, I ask them if I can sleep next to them on the futon in their bedroom. I say that the backrest will help to support my body, my aching bones. The truth is I feel afraid, for reasons I don't fully understand; I want to be close to them. I watch my mother as she checks the stove, the lights, the locks on all the doors. Before turning off the lights, my mother locks the bedroom door. *Why do you lock it?* I ask. *To be safe, lang,* she says. I lie awake, hearing the creaks of the walls and floors. I know it's the house, its memories and complaints, but I feel uneasy. Then, I hear my mother's quiet snore and a puff of air from my father's lips. These are the sounds of them entering sleep, locked away, safe and peaceful, in their home in the suburbs of Biddle City.

Highway Haiku

I stop twice and speak to the folks I meet in crisp Midwestern English.

My Therapist Talks About Biddle City

She asks why I'm here, and I say, *I'm having a biracial child, and I'm afraid she'll be white.* This is a rapid-access telehealth call. My therapist's face is framed by a rectangle inside a rectangle on my computer. My therapist is a white person. She squints as she listens, never interrupts. I say I'm afraid my child will reject me, choose my partner's family, my partner's personality, because he's white and this country is white. My therapist asks if I grew up in Biddle City. *There are lots of Biddle Cities everywhere,* she tells me. I didn't know she knew about Biddle City. I thought it was a place that I made up. I realize what was wrong all along. I say, *I'm not a biracial person, but I'm afraid that I'm white. I'm afraid that I made myself white. That I'd chosen whiteness a long time ago.* I see myself crying on a square on my computer screen. Like this, my face looks undeniably Asian. I try to relax so that it is no longer crumpled in this way, but it doesn't move. It's frozen like this, in its rectangular box.

Autobiography via Forgetting

1.

I once heard someone call themselves *a string of memories*. The opposite is true for me. I'm a cement block of forgetfulness. For every new memory, something else gets lost or disfigured: a recipe for lentils, dance moves, someone's birthday, names of directors, actors. I manage to get them all wrong. Some people claim that they've retained memories from past lives. I can't remember what happened in this one.

2.

Most of my childhood is gone from my brain. I ask my brother questions, and we sort out what we know. I say, *But didn't we?* And he says, *I think that was someone else.* The thing I remember most is the blue feeling in my chest as a child, that sudden gloom. My dad told me that he spoke to a colonel he worked for in the nineties. The colonel remembered me as *the child who used to cry all the time.* I don't remember crying all the time, but it's possible I did because I forgot that I was safe and happy.

3.

I read somewhere that memory is not stored as it is on a hard drive. Instead, it is something you recreate in each version of remembering. It is a process of sculpting. Perhaps, the difference between memory and imagination is simply the clay you use.

4.

When I was about eight or nine (or six or seven?) I asked my mother to please give me another sibling. It was not that my brother wasn't enough, but I wanted to be the middle child, to sit between two bodies where I could be securely tucked away. This child would be another brain for our family, another memory-maker. My parents said no, didn't even try! So I remained the youngest in my family, a flea clinging to the tip of our animal tail. We don't know and will never know what that third child could've remembered that we've all now forgotten.

5.

In my early twenties, I had a boyfriend who asked me if I ever forgot I was a racial minority. I said, *Yes, I forget everything.* But of course, it was a stupid answer to a stupid question. I mean, who walks around thinking all the time: *I'm a minority, I'm a minority.*

6.

There are places in the US like Daly City in northern California where more than half the people are Asian, where cultures and languages from nations of origin are kept strong. This is all to say: People of color in America experience moments of majority. In the Midwest, at a Filipino gathering for example, I am awash in majorityness. In this room where I am alone, I am majority. And in my body, my spirit takes up more space than any other spirit. The majority of me is me, while the minority of me is me as a minority.

7.

What does it mean to forget something really? When I am asked to speak Cebuano, my parents' language, I struggle to put two words together. Certain words don't flake off the tongue like stewed meat from bone. But when I hear Cebuano spoken, I understand its meanings. The language is there in the mind behind a closed door, key dangling from the knob. I only have access to the meanings when someone else turns the key. It is the same as me remembering that I am a racial minority. When some external thing reminds me is when I know it most fully.

8.

Now, in my thirties, despite the state of the world, I want a baby. I want to hold a new memory-maker against my chest like fragile glass. It amazes me how strong the desire is. S. tells me to forget about it. *Don't think, don't write, don't talk about it*, she says, *and it'll happen.* And yet, I cannot resist writing about it. And yet, sometimes I say *baby* to myself as I fall asleep with my ear against my cat's ribs, her purrs buzzing against my head. *My baby.*

9.

One cannot try to forget something without remembering it. Emily Dickinson writes, *Heart, we will forget him! / You and I, to-night!* and yet, *he* is in the poem, immortalized like the beloved in Shakespeare's "Sonnet 18." And in this poem that I am writing, my beloved is forgetfulness. Forgetting is remembered, immortalized *so long as men can breathe or eyes can see.* To get me to fall asleep, my father used to tell me to think of nothing. Tell someone not to think, and the brain will run wild. The mind is fiddly that way. The mind is only manipulated by trickery: sheep counting, body scans, a catalogue of the things you don't remember.

Filipina Universe (Biddle City Filipina, No. 3)

I forget sometimes that we are ancient and holy.

That we walked across land bridges with Pleistocene mammals to find shelter on an island.

At least, someone once imagined that we did. And this story is a part of us, myth with mammoths and mastodon.

Before the Spanish arrived, broad faces and flat noses were beautiful in our universe. We molded our babies' skulls using rods bound to their foreheads.

If our skulls were unmolded, we were called *ondo*, which meant *tight-packed or overstuffed.*

We are ondo now, overstuffed, our heads round, our bodies heavy as we circle one another, as we dance in a straight line.

*

I think about you dancing the electric slide our synchronized movements. *You can't see it. (It's electric!) You gotta feel it. (It's electric!)*

When *you* means *I*, everything multiplies.

When *you* means *we*, the branches grow limes on a Midwestern tree with surprising ferocity, not limoncitos, but big universes of green.

When *we* means *we*, it is both truth and lie. Do we want the same things?

Notice our synchrony.

In astronomy, synchrony refers to a celestial body completing one full revolution around another while the body being orbited completes a full rotation about its axis.

It is like being here with you, happenstance.

It is a dance, little bulbs of universe swinging on a grapevine. It is the grapevine.

See me turning as I circle around you. Do I ever see your face?

*

And we move, we migrate, we dance. We wanted

out. We wrote letters and married men who live across the ocean, men who lived in snow.

We rode a plane to be with them. We worried they would kill us. We wore our jeans in bed at night, because that was what the embassy told us to do.

We wore our jeans in bed. We kept our passports in our back pocket.

We were ready to run if something happened, if the men we married were to become killers.

Some of us were given life insurance, our bodies were sent back to the Philippines

because of the husbands we had.

We knew to wear our jeans in bed, hold our passports close.

Our husbands call their friends on the phone *I don't know what to do with my wife, she's wearing jeans in bed.*

We laugh about it now.

We are lucky when our husbands are not killers. We are lucky. Our husbands talk to people with black hair at Meijer while shopping. Our husbands ask them if they're Filipino. We ask our husbands *Do you think every person with black hair is a Filipino?* And they say *I just want you to have friends.* Our husbands say *If you want something? If you want something?* And we learn to love them.

*

Inside our bones, an ache. The ache escapes me when I am around you, when I am you, you inside me, when we are *we*, here, together, our selves forgotten, dancing

in a straight line: the hustle, todo-todo, cupid shuffle, cha-cha slide.

We knew one day we'd become singular selves.

We already knew as children the possibilities of distance, our mothers away from their mothers, our lolas die, and we are years and years away, centuries, an expansive field of time. Years of light, light-years away.

Remember our years of light? We cradled our skulls, sculpting ourselves into something new.

*

We decorated our teeth and bodies. We grew our hair long. We prided in great masses of hair, oil-sweet-scented. We ran

our fingers over our children's scalps, oiling their skulls, wrapping their heads in cloth. We oiled our daughters' feet

and legs. We kissed their feet and legs. We bathed ourselves in warm water. We smelled of sesame oil. We appeared

slick from the water onto the sand, legs emerging so that we could run, if needed. Run anywhere.

*

And we learned how to hold ourselves and each other, to restore function, relieve ache. We leave our island to become

therapists for each other.

*

And I couldn't tell you what waited across the ocean.

Where the branches grow fruit on a Midwestern tree with surprising ferocity—not lansones, not caimito—big universes of green.

And I couldn't tell you what Michigan was.

We had no idea. We just knew, at the time, in the early nineties, the Detroit Pistons were the champions, so we said we want to go there to watch Isiah Thomas.

We drove everywhere, all over Michigan, then some parts of Arkansas, then Missouri. It was adventure. All our income we gave to the telephone company because we called home all the time.

Our first assignment was in the Flint area. We traveled alone.

Most of our clients were old. In their sixties, Medicare patients. One time I met a patient

who didn't want to work with me because they, or their father, fought against the Filipinos in a war. (I can't remember which one.) I said I was not born then.

We ended up working together. He was apologetic. I told him, no, it doesn't affect me

because my conscience is clear, we did not cause the war.

We learned that as long as you have gas in your car and a map and it's daylight—

ask directions from gas stations. We didn't have GPS, we didn't have cell phone. The only thing that gave us company was a Rand McNally, a big book of maps. That was the only life we knew we had to do.

*

And when it snows   we know how

To navigate the roads   to shovel

Our driveway   we pave

A way   pump my brakes   over ice.

*

And don't you remember during the war? Petrified of snakes—it was our job to feed the chickens

in the chicken coops far away from the cave where we lived.

This one day we were singing, hopping and singing, and going our merry way, and then we stopped.

The chicken was gone. In its place was a huge python, and the reason why the python was in the chicken coop is because he swallowed the chicken and couldn't get out.

We ran back to our grandfather, and said *The chicken, the chicken.*

And he said *What happened to the chicken.* And we said *Gone, gone.*

We couldn't talk. He had to shake us. And we never found out what happened to the snake, but the chicken was gone. The snake swallowed it. We were petrified.

Here in Michigan, we planted garlic with our flowers. Because we saw a garter snake once, and so we have to plant garlic, among the flowers and vegetables. Everywhere.

The first year that we were here, we could not afford to buy a washer and dryer. So we bought a washing machine, and Mila hung the clothes in the basement.

And then Tony bought a ten-inch TV, from his student.

We didn't have two nickels to rub together, okay? We were the only ones working while he goes to school.

When we were in the Philippines, we had five dogs, a cat, a white parrot, a green parrot, and two parakeets, and when it's feeding time, our house sounded like a zoo. The dog is barking, the cat is meowing, the parrots are yakking

because they want food too. But when we arrived here,

we couldn't afford a pet. We got home from work one day and Tony Jr. reached into his flannel jacket and pulled out

a garter snake. And we were petrified of snakes, and so we ran upstairs. And Tony was of course in our bedroom studying. We said *You're coming with us or not?*

And he said *Where are we going?*

And we said *To a pet shop to order a dog.* We could not afford to buy a dryer, but we paid $350 to buy a dog. Now, figure that one out.

But then, we could just imagine him marching down the stairs, and that stupid snake going around our ankles. We're petrified of snakes. Think how big the python was. Big as a house.

*

And sometimes—in the universe of the community center—we create
a circle with our bodies,

and one of us dances in the middle of it.

Sometimes she moves her arms into the shape of an ocean.

Sometimes she hugs herself, holding herself, shy and afraid.

Sometimes she lifts her hands up and gyrates.

Sometimes she rotates

all the way around so that she can see all our faces.

*

And in a universe that we perceive as almost flat, we flatten our heads, broaden our noses,

and we make circles.

We shape balls of dough into pandesal (salt bread), from the Spanish colonial pan de suelo (floor bread), but softer, doughier, better

for dipping in morning coffee.

We ball our hands into fists, and sometimes, feeling unable to fight the python-as-big-as-the-house, we fight

our children, we're hard on them, then loving, then hard on them, then loving. Sometimes we circle each other in chismis, and then, we become tired

of all the chismis, and we go back to making bread and meatballs and leaving round fruit for our ancestors.

The chismis satisfied our need for story, but only for a short while, for what we craved were storytellers, a circle of story, a story told in circles, a story of circles.

We turned on the karaoke machine, and we sang sad songs.

We danced the electric slide. We worshipped Isiah Thomas.

And in a universe that we perceive as almost flat, flat as a trampoline, sometimes we ball our hands into fists and rub the backs of our children before bed, and they massage our tired feet, and they press hard, sometimes it hurts us, but we forgive them.

We write poems that go round and round.

We drive round and round. We look at maps, trying to find ourselves inside a grid.

We mix together sweet rice flour and shredded coconut, roll them into balls, fry them, and prick them with skewers.

We roll small pieces of dough, fry them, and add sesame seeds.

We suck on the round seeds of lansones, because roundness is medicinal, roundness is wealth and good fortune, and seeds are both endings and beginnings.

Lakephrasis

After Harry Callahan's *Lake Michigan, 1954* and
Sunlight on Water, 1943

Impossible that I was born from Lake Michigan, that I would emerge from the water like a beaching newborn North American whitefish.

No, my family arrived from elsewhere, wanting to build a home where we could clap away the dust from our travels.

Not documentary photography. Not the sharp double exposures created by rewinding the film.

The feeling was more akin to motion, photograph called *Sunlight on Water*, the smoke-ring momentum, the telephone poles rising behind the fog.

And I wondered all that time how I would ever belong in this place, how could I ever make art here, unable to swim inside these abstract forms of light and shadow, but somehow, we took our clothes off, dug our feet into the sand.

At times the weather was perfect for soaking.

Sometimes I am lonely for my idea of Lake Michigan, a place to bathe and come out cleaner than I was.

The Children

The children are still locked out of their duplex
apartment and sitting on the front steps.
I see them there now. Time has moved away,
but they've stayed, locked in place.
Father is due to arrive before Mother at four thirty.
The day is a newly mowed lawn, or a military
haircut, which is to say it has lost its curl,
the back and sides shaved to the skin.
They amuse themselves by tying their shoes
into byzantine knots and telling each other
Truths. The brother is in love with an Erin
or a Haley, and the sister wonders, all the time,
if she herself is worthy of friendship.
In their neighbor's backyard is a cheap trampoline
that's lost its bounce glimmering in the full light
of the afternoon. It rained the day before,
and tree pollen floats in the water that pools
on rarely-used deck furniture. This is the suburbs
in June, and all the neighborhood kids
are sitting in front of their televisions. *What time
is it now*, the sister asks. Still, they sit like statues.
They mostly get along, but sometimes
they hit each other until one of them cries
or pees their pants. Sometimes the brother
remembers something, and the sister pretends
to remember, says *I was there too*, even if
she wasn't. A loose cat walks by, a rare sight
where they live, and separately and together
they wonder how it might feel to stray.

Notes

"Biddle City High School Theatre Kids" is dedicated to Phil Ashbrook, Samantha Seybert, and Justin Garascia.

In "Autobiography via Revision," the information about Biddle City comes from the "Lansing, Michigan" Wikipedia page (July 2020) and from Emanuele Berry's 2013 interview with David Votta on WKAR. At the time of the interview, David Votta was the Community Engagement Librarian at the Midwest Collaborative for Library Services.

The text from "A Revision" comes from an article about Biddle City published in the *Lansing State Journal* on Sunday, March 20, 1955.

The Russian text in "Let's Talk for a Moment" is the beginning of Aleksandr Pushkin's "Winter Morning." The following is Ivan Panin's translation of these lines to English: "Frost and sun—the day is wondrous! / Thou still art slumbering, charming friend."

The final section of "Autobiography via Forgetting" contains quotations from Emily Dickinson's "Heart, we will forget him!" and William Shakespeare's "Sonnet 18."

Some of the language from the "Biddle City Filipina" series and from some of "Filipina Universe (Biddle City Filipina, No. 3)" comes from interviews I conducted between 2022 and 2023 with three Filipinas living in Michigan. When I lived in Michigan, the Filipino community in the Lansing metro area was mostly made up of women who immigrated to the States for marriage or employment opportunities. My goals for these conversations were to better understand the forces that brought these women to the Midwest and gain insight into their experiences here. What was it like to move here in the seventies, eighties, and nineties? How does one muster up the courage to start a new life in a new place? In doing these interviews and writing these poems, I learned more than I expected about the bravery and generosity within my small Midwestern Filipino community. I learned about the particularities and complexities of these women's lives that I hadn't learned before because I never asked. I hope to continue learning more about my community beyond the publication of this book. The women I interviewed asked to remain anonymous. Please note that because the language is taken directly from the interviews, different Englishes appear in these poems, and I wished to honor the differences in speech.

"Filipina Universe (Biddle City Filipina, No. 3)" was inspired by Robin Coste Lewis's *To the Realization of Perfect Helplessness*, published from Alfred A. Knopf in 2022.

Descriptions of precolonial Visayan practices in "Filipina Universe (Biddle City Filipina, No. 3)" comes from William Henry Scott's *Barangay: Sixteenth-Century Philippine Culture and Society*, published from Ateneo de Manila University Press in 1994.

Acknowledgments

Thank you to the following journals, where many of these poems first appeared:

AGNI, "The Shape of Biddle City," "Summer in Biddle City, 1999"
Ambit, "Summer in Biddle City, 2000," "Summer in Biddle City, 2001"
American Literary Review, "The Great Recession," "A Visit to the
  Suburbs, 2021"
Boulevard, "Love Song for Kien"
DIAGRAM, "The Biddle City Musical," "Leaving Biddle City"
The Journal, "Lakephrasis"
Kenyon Review, "Biddle City Filipina, No. 1," "The Walnut House,"
  "Let's Talk for a Moment," "Autobiography via Forgetting,"
Poetry, "Love Song for Ayumi," "My Therapist Talks About Biddle
  City"
The Ex-Puritan, "Winter Flowers in Biddle City," "Falling in Love with
  Biddle City"
Southern Indiana Review, "Autobiography via Screaming"

"Autobiography via Forgetting" was reprinted in *Pushcart Prize XLVII: Best of the Small Presses 2023*, edited by Bill Henderson.

"The Shape of Biddle City" was reprinted in the 2023 edition of *Best American Poetry*, edited by David Lehman and Elaine Equi.

"The Walnut House" was reprinted in the Sarabande anthology *Another Last Call: Poems on Addiction & Deliverance*, edited by Kaveh Akbar and Paige Lewis.

Here is my litany of gratitude:

Thank you to the folks at Sarabande Books—Sarah, Kristen, Danika, Natalie, and Joanna—for believing in this book. Thank you to Emma for your sharp copyeditor's eye.

I'm grateful to the following artists for inspiring or responding to the poems in this collection: Lisa Low, Danni Quintos, Su Cho, Anni Liu, Luisa A. Igloria, Olivia Friedman, Geoff Bouvier, Jessica Q. Stark, Kien Lam, Nicholas Molbert, Taylor Byas, Connor Yeck, Madeleine Wattenberg, Matthew Yeager, Cara Dees, Yalie Kamara, Paige Webb, Holli Carrell, Leila Chatti, Colleen Mayo, Eleanor Boudreau, Josh Wild, Tanya Grae, Dorsey Craft, and Lee Patterson.

I began writing this collection during the COVID-19 lockdown, and I wouldn't have been able to write anything without the support, inspiration, and artistic exchange that occurred during Thursday night Zoom poker from 2020 to 2021 with SJ Sindu, Geoff Bouvier, Daniel Tysdal, David Brock, Clancy McGilligan, and others.

Thank you to my teachers at the University of Cincinnati: Rebecca Lindenberg, John Drury, Aditi Machado, Felicia Zamora, and Jenn Glaser for your endless guidance and support. For encouraging me to go deep. For encouraging me to play.

Thank you to my colleagues at Old Dominion University: Jane Alberdeston, Luisa A. Igloria, John McManus, and Kent Wascom. I'm so lucky to be able to work with you.

Thank you to the folks at Kundiman. Thank you to Filipino and Asian American communities everywhere.

Thank you to my parents, Jack and Patricia, for your unwavering love and support.

Thank you to Clancy McGilligan, my love, my anchor, my light.

Thank you to Inez, my sweetness, my wonder.

Thank you to my brother, Rammel—the funniest guy, my lifelong best friend. This book is for you.

Sarabande Books is a nonprofit independent literary press headquartered in Louisville, Kentucky. Established in 1994 to champion poetry, fiction, and essay, we are committed to creating lasting editions that honor exceptional writing. With over two hundred titles in print, we have earned a dedicated readership and a national reputation as a publisher of diverse forms and innovative voices.

Marianne Chan grew up in Stuttgart, Germany, and Lansing, Michigan. She is the author of *All Heathens* (Sarabande Books, 2020), which was the winner of the 2021 GLCA New Writers Award in Poetry, the 2021 Ohioana Book Award in Poetry, and the 2022 Association for Asian American Studies Book Award in Poetry. Her poems have appeared in *Poetry, New England Review, Kenyon Review, Michigan Quarterly Review*, and elsewhere. A Kundiman Fellow, she holds an MFA in Creative Writing from the University of Nevada, Las Vegas, and a PhD in Creative Writing and Literature from the University of Cincinnati. Chan is an assistant professor of English at Old Dominion University in Norfolk, Virginia.